MARCUS & CALLEY PRESENT:

Big Big Topics
for
Little Little Kids

Written By CLAUDETTE McGOWAN • Artwork By HONEY PEARL PELAEZ

Library and Archives Canada Cataloguing in Publication

McGowan, Claudette
Big big topics for little little kids / written by Claudette McGowan ; artwork by Honey Pearl Pelaez. -- 2nd ed.
At head of title: Marcus & Calley present.

ISBN 978-0-9812114-3-5

1. Children--Conduct of life--Juvenile poetry. I. Pelaez, Honey Pearl II. Title. III. Title: Marcus & Calley present Big big topics for little little kids.

PS8625.G68B53 2012   jC811'.6   C2012-903742-7

Editing by Trecia K. McLennon
Cover & Interior Design by Justine Elliott
Artwork by Honey Pearl Pelaez

Excelovate

P.O. Box 34021
RPO Hollandview #7
Aurora, Ontario
L4G 0G3

Dedication

To parents, teachers, guardians and kids committed to open and honest communication.

My name is Marcus.

My name is Calley.

And we live in a big, big city.

We have lots of friends, and loving parents.

But sometimes life is not so pretty.

We have some stories
we wish to share.

About family, friends, school and life.

We hope our stories help all kids.

With ups and downs,
and joys and strife.

Read these stories with your Mommy.

With your Daddy, and your close friend.

Listen, learn and enjoy the messages.

From Marcus and Calley,
your pals to the end.

Rhymes for Our Times

- Our Growing Family
- Neighbourhood Safety
- Bully Proof
- Talking Helps
- Happy Parents - Happy Home
- Celebrating Differences

Our Growing Family

My Mommy's getting fatter
Her tummy is so big
She's smaller than a cow
But bigger than a pig

Every time I see her
She's eating, eating, eating
I guess she quit her diet
Or maybe she's just cheating

My parents sat me down
Their faces filled with joy
They told me to be happy
Mommy's pregnant with a boy

At first I felt so happy
And then I felt so sad
The baby might replace me
No more time with Mom or Dad

Daddy told me not to worry
We'll always have great fun
And they never will replace me
Because I am their number one!

Neighbourhood
Safety

Never talk to strangers
You don't know who they are

Never answer their questions
And don't ever go in their car

A stranger may try to trick you
With sweet candies or a pup

Keep far away from these strangers
And stay close to a grown-up

An adult that you know and love
Will keep you away from danger

So always remember the golden rule
Is to never talk to a stranger.

Bully Proof

Bullies are super-meanies
They'll pick on you and fight

Bullies are not too friendly
They don't behave quite right

A bully may try to push you
Or call you some bad names

They won't be fair when playing
You can bet they'll cheat in games

A bully may swipe your lunch money
And act like a very mean creature

The best way to deal with a bully
Is to tell your parents or teacher.

Talking Helps

There are many people around us
Some are good and some are bad

Some want to make us smile
Others want to make us sad

If there is a person
That is causing you some pain

Tell everybody around you
Be bold! Do not refrain

Tell your mother, tell your father
Tell your friends and tell your teacher

Tell your auntie and your uncle
Tell your priest or tell your preacher

No one should put a hand on you
Be sure and tell someone if they do

They can't hurt you once you tell
Don't keep quiet - you must yell!

Happy Parents - Happy Home

We have to cheer up Johnny
Lately, he's been sad
His parents are always fighting
And his Mommy is very mad

His Daddy wants to move
And plans to leave the home
Now Johnny can't stop crying
Because he feels so all alone

Let's explain that problems happen
Everyone hurts when there is strain
Johnny needs a listening ear
To help him through his pain

Johnny says he feels so small
Like a tiny grain of salt
He thinks his parents problems
Must be all his fault

Let's remind him that he's precious
Like a heavenly little dove
Johnny always must remember
We never lose our parents love.

Celebrating Differences

We have a friend born in India
Another friend born in Spain

We know a boy from Zimbabwe
That now lives down the lane

Dimitra goes to Greek school
Mary Catherine goes to Mass

Avi visits his Synagogue
Maria skips to Spanish class

Delroy is from Jamaica
Marie Claude was born in France

LaToya is from Trinidad
She loves to sing and dance

We all have different
backgrounds
That's what makes our
friendships great

And nothing will come
between us
Because we are filled
with love - not hate.

Until Next Time

We hope you enjoyed our stories

There are many more stories to share

We wish you joy and happiness

Because we really, really care!

Your Pals,
Marcus & Calley